BEHIND THE CURTAIN

TALES OF AN INTREPID TRAVELLER

Peggy Haswell

Published by

MELROSE BOOKS

An Imprint of Melrose Press Limited
St Thomas Place, Ely
Cambridgeshire
CB7 4GG, UK
www.melrosebooks.co.uk

FIRST EDITION

Cover by Melrose Books

ISBN   978-1-911280-57-6
epub   978-1-911280-58-3
mobi   978-1-911280-59-0

Printed and bound in Great Britain by:
Berforts South West Limited
17 Burgess Road
Hastings
East Sussex
TN35 4NR

Dedicated to Shirley Gratwick

As I am approaching one hundred years of age, I am no longer able to type. This book, *Behind the Curtain*, has been typed by Christina Walford with my appreciative thanks.

Other books published by Melrose Books
by this author

Through High Water and Low: My Unusual Travels
ISBN 9781907040184

Contents

Chapter 1

Our Siamese Cat is Missing

It was the first village fete since before the dark years of war, and the crowd was filled with excitement. When one of the charity women came before me and asked me to buy a ticket, I bought one, pocketed it and thought no more about it. At the end of the day, tickets were drawn, and to my amazement, I had won first prize. It was a Siamese kitten and off we ran to the manor to collect it.

We were given a beautiful, striking blue-eyed kitten. She was terrified and rushed around in a panic, up and down the curtains. But she soon settled and became a much loved part of the family.

A year later, disaster happened. She went missing during another fete. We searched and searched for many days but we never found her. When, one evening, we heard a faint cry at our door and opened it, there she was, tragically thin, her paws bleeding; she was in a most terrible state.

Meanwhile, we had bought a dog – a lovely cocker spaniel. No way could they live together, and in the end, we had to let the dog go and gave it to a local farmer. It reminded us of the recent sadness following the war.

Many airman and soldiers back from the war discovered their wives had taken a new man. A colleague during my time in Africa had a similar experience shortly after the war. On coming home, he learned that his wife had found another man. He then left England for Africa once again, but could never recover from his despair at the loss of his wife. He worked in the most difficult parts of Africa, without respite, and was soon seriously ill.

But in our English family at home, the Siamese cat happily lived on for seventeen years, while the dog had been rather miserable.

Chapter 2

Constable at the Gate

I had been freed from six years in a reserved occupation during the war, and I was excited at the thought of flying off to Africa.

The plane was a converted wartime Dakota and the first stop was to be in France. We were eleven passengers, fully occupying the plane, and as we descended into Bordeaux, it struck a pile of metal sheets and crashed – nose-diving into the airstrip. A General sitting at the front of the plane cried out: "Stop speaking all of you!" but none of us were speaking; we had all been quite shocked and were hanging in odd shapes from our seatbelts. Fortunately, no one was injured. However, as I was trapped in the tail end of the plane, a crane had to be brought to get me out. A French lady waiting to board the plane was so frightened she just got up and went home.

It was Labour Day in France and not a shop was open, and we spent a dreary twenty-four hours in a rather poor hotel, waiting for another plane to be sent for us. We touched down in the North African desert for refuelling. Six men with multi-coloured feathers on their heads, and nothing much else on them, appeared at the side of the plane, refuelling it with hand-held cans. We then continued on at fairly low speed until we arrived at Bathurst in Gambia, landing on terrifying metal sheets, which created a dreadful noise. We were then told to identify our baggage, which was sitting on a bench in the open.

I met the other two of our particular three pioneers, and the next day we acquired a lorry and filled it with food and a forty-gallon drum containing water. The day after, we set off into primeval forest to reach a village about one-hundred miles into the interior. Six local people walked ahead of us, slashing and cutting forest debris to help us travel, and after some hours, we reached a river. A boat, large enough to contain our lorry, was by the bank and we travelled across using hand ropes. As we travelled, looking over into the water, we saw a great number of very nasty crocodiles.

On arriving at the village, we were stopped by a large gorilla that had been trained to guard the entrance. Eventually, it let us pass, quite luckily. As we entered, behold, a number of local women ran away. They were frightened to death of white-skinned people. Slowly, we began to explain our presence. We told them that we had been sent to find out how these remote African villagers lived. Among our three people, the man was a medic and the other woman a nutritionist. I was an agronomist.

We set ourselves up in local huts and began to study the lives of the villagers. Soon after, as we sat in the early evening outside one of our huts, drinking beer that we had brought with us, we suddenly saw a snake slithering through the thatched roof of the hut ahead. A very large, green snake. Fortunately, our medic had his gun, and he shot it, which went 'flop' in front of us. The medic stretched it out and measured it – seventeen feet. It was a poisonous snake – a killer.

I later went by river back to Bathurst to collect some equipment. On returning, the boat, which was a government launch, broke down near our village area. The captain asked us to get out of the launch and into a fishing dugout, which happened to be on the river nearby. We were to take it up the creek to warn the village and get them to send a messenger to the government launch's normal stop. I had with me one of our locals, and we got off the boat, into the dugout, and the new boatman set us off with a single oar. The dugout got stuck in the mud as we entered the creek, and all three of us got out to push it free. The African with me said, "You must get back into the boat because you have white legs and the crocodiles will get you." So I got back into the boat, and the boatman and the local struggled to push it off the mud, and then we were able to enter the creek. To his astonishment, our medic saw us emerging. The African took our equipment, purchased in Bathurst, on his head, and we walked off the creek towards our huts. Suddenly, he shrieked with terrible screams – it was a dreadful situation. Our local African had been stung by a scorpion on his foot.

It was approaching Christmas, and the medic's wife and two infant children arrived. After Christmas, I had to go back again to England to obtain some equipment. It was on this return to the village that there had been a crisis. Both the medic and the nutritionist had flown.

Chapter 3

Lonely Aftermath

It occurred to me that I should seek help from the District Officer, who was resident a few miles further into the forest interior. I now had a jeep, and off I went. He was a charming man and we had a very good relationship.

On the way back, I approached the creek and had a horrifying shock halfway across. A very large crocodile, which the villagers had been worried about, rose out the water right in front of my jeep and then rested his whole body across the creek. I knew that if he noticed me, he could knock the jeep down and swallow me up. I thought that if I kept the jeep running, the smell of the petrol might cause him to want to leave it and get back into the creek. For a full fifteen minutes, I sat perfectly still, looking at his huge body heaving up and down as he breathed. Suddenly, he started to move. His huge body was gradually leaving the water, the tail coming along across the creek, and then with an enormous splash, he was gone. I was so relieved.

The District Officer, all on his own a few miles away, could give me no help. The rains were coming, and the time was approaching for the beginning of the new crop season when another dreadful crisis occurred, this time with dire consequences. One of the village youths, about twelve-years old, had been stung by a scorpion and was rapidly poisoned. The villagers called the magician. The magician mixed in a bowl his own strange medicines and filled it with water. Stirring very thoroughly, he then poured it slowly into the dying boy's mouth, speaking at the same time a number of unintelligible words. Then, when the boy had finally finished the bowl, he died.

For several months, I was left alone in the village with absolutely no contacts, but I had my African assistant, and together we went through the 1948 rains, the crop and the harvest.

Then came a young European researching birds, and it was the beginning of a flood of visitors. Dean had come out to Africa as his wife had left him during the war, and he was in despair. He stayed on and helped the villagers prepare for the new season and I fell in love with him and we had a brief affair.

Meanwhile, John had arrived as my permanent assistant. He had left behind his wife and baby because the baby had eczema and could not immediately fly. But before Christmas, John's wife, Shirley, and their five-month-old baby, Jane, arrived, and they went off to the coast to spend the holidays together. Again, I was alone among the villagers, but to my amazement, a lorry arrived, fantastically decorated. Inside were a number of candles, and around the sides of the lorry, a number of magical figures and curious, brilliantly painted objects. This was their way of celebrating Christmas, travelling along from village to village, into the interior. By the end of 1949, my contract with the Colonial Government had ended, and unwilling to renew it, I left, as did John and Shirley, with baby Jane.

Chapter 4

Never Run in Terror

I was back in Africa, this time to the South East, in a remote area where rainfall was no more than four inches a year – far too little for growing any crops. The British Government, short of fats after the war, sent technicians to the area, mistakenly, to grow crops, which of course were a total failure. I was sent to rescue anything that remained in the area, and in the course of this, I had to go and visit the District Officer who was a few miles further into the forest.

On the return, the jeep's local driver stopped, took out the key and disappeared. There I was, left alone in the jeep, with scary creatures making worrying noises round and about. After an hour or so, thankfully, he reappeared, this time carrying, on his head, a bed mattress. He had apparently gone to some kind of hut that was his own home. On we went for about two hours, when he stopped again. I asked him why he had stopped, and he simply turned his head to the right, and there I saw a lion, a lioness and three babies, right by the jeep. I tried to get him to move on, but he wouldn't and I had to get out instead. I saw far in the distance a single light, and I began to run towards it, very stupidly, because there were creatures around who obviously thought, *what is that silly creature running?*, but they did not attack. I found, in the hut, a gamekeeper on his own, and he said, "You stay here and I will go and sort out the driver, who should have carried on."

Chapter 5

A Faraway Golden Dream

By now I was a university lecturer in tropical economics, in countries that were ten degrees north and ten degrees south of the equator. But I had yet to visit the subcontinent of India. I travelled on a large plane from London filled with big Indian men. On arrival at Delhi Airport, a long line of Indians were passing through customs, and I was the last passenger arrival. On appearing at customs, the Indian officials were astonished to find this unimportant English woman.

The hotel was occupied entirely by males, and it was not British – they thought that a woman should not be moving about the hotel on her own. It was my intention to travel far south to Madras, but first I wanted to go the short distance to Agra.

At Agra I had been invited to stay in the house of a senior resident and found, at dinner in the evening, some fifty guests. After an incredible meal we were then given beds outside on a very large landing. Before six in the morning, I was taken by the host and an assistant to visit the Taj Mahal as the sun rose, and there we were, at the far end of a magnificent drive, in the rising sun. We saw the wonderful Taj Mahal, one of the Seven Wonders of the World. Later that morning, I returned to Delhi and began my long trek to Madras.

En route I spent a night in Bombay and finally reached Madras, travelling in a small plane. I arrived on a grassy runway and saw a single lady waiting. The lady was the young person I was joining to travel with among the villages in that part of India.

An Indian lady, she was in the employ of the University of Madras, where women were not allowed to travel out of the institution. She said, straight away to me, "We must hurry and escape the university seniors, who will stop us going to the villages." And so we went quickly to the railway station and boarded a train to one of the villages she had decided to go. When we reached the village, it was late and dark, and we were the only passengers to leave the train. There we sat on a bench, waiting and waiting and waiting. I did not know quite what we were waiting for, until a mule with a cart slowly arrived to collect us. We climbed into the cart, which had some straw lining the bed, and sat down. Slowly it jogged along for about two or three hours when, suddenly, we saw the village – right there was a large sign which said 'Welcome'.

I was given a hut, while my Indian companion was taken away and given a splendid feast. For me, they brought up a tray with some food on it. Finally, we set off again to reach the next village, and here we had a far less fortune. We were immediately shut up in the local prison for the night – under lock and key. My Indian companion was terrified, and I spent the night trying to console her, though I was not sure whether they would unlock us in the morning. They did. As we left we watched a long line of women waiting to pass through, one by one, a wooden building. As they emerged, the women were screaming and crying. They had destroyed their ability to have children. My companion was distressed to see the downtrodden and agonised women in this village. On and on we went from village to village, each having its own crisis, until at last we reached the far-eastern end of the state.

Being rather exhausted, we then decided to return back to Madras and took a night train.

Arriving back at Madras, we were confronted by senior men who said they were staggered to hear of our adventure. "We never go to the villages," they said. I said goodbye to Madras and took a train on my way along the East of India.

Chapter 6

A Hair-Raising Attack

I had left Madras and was travelling up Eastern India. Part of the way, I left the train to visit two English people living in the country. They were growing tobacco and were very saddened that they had to leave India, which had been freed from Colonial Britain for only thirteen years. But India was calling the Brits to pack it up now and go home. I returned to the railway station and continued my journey.

I was approaching the remote interior, where primitive people lived. At the edge of the area I hired a car, but the local Indian interpreters insisted that I should have two cars because of tigers, and they were worried that one might attack a single vehicle. Happily, we travelled far, into a village, without seeing a single tiger, and we spent a fascinating time hearing how the villagers lived.

On our way back to the hut where we had left our things, we did not see a tiger, but we were apprehended, to our amazement, by soldiers. Our second car panicked and rushed away, and the interpreter with me grabbed the key from our car to stop the driver, who also wanted to escape. Seventeen soldiers were sitting round the bed in the hut where I was sleeping. Three soldiers were outside waiting for us. Our interpreter and I were lent across the wall of the hut and questioned. What immediately worried me, was that the senior solider demanded my passport. As he took my passport I became really frightened. Without my passport I thought I would never be able to get out of India. My interpreter started a fearful argument and eventually managed to get the passport back. But the soldiers intended to spend the night in the hut, and my interpreter and I took the other room and waited all night, anxiously, until the morning came. My interpreter was a wonderful man who finally got us away and back into normal India, as it seemed to me. Here we parted company, and I took a train to Calcutta.

Calcutta was seething with people, whole families living on pavements. I had been invited by a small group of English traders who had yet to leave the country, but when the gentleman opened the door to me, he refused to let me in. My hair was a dreadful mess and my clothes in considerable need of a change. So I went out into the street in search of a hairdresser, passing by whole families living on the streets, and finally found a shop. After having my hair done and generally transforming myself, I went back and was accepted. Here was Europe – or a mirage of Europe in the middle of India. There were a few ladies and gentlemen, and the arrangements inside were incredibly rich in a sense. One lady played the piano, another sang. They offered me a lovely meal, and they gave me a room for the night, which was incredibly comfortable. I then left them and went to the airport. I took a flight out of Calcutta and out of India.

Chapter 7

Oasis in a Sea of Turbulence

Bangkok, the capital city of Thailand, welcomes people from all over the world; Thailand has kept itself successfully uninvaded by other cultures or colonised by bordering countries. I spent a day and night in Bangkok before moving up country. At breakfast, alone in the hotel (there were no other visitors), I was circled by three Tia waitresses. These Tia waitresses were watching me have breakfast. So extraordinary, they thought, to eat breakfast with a knife and fork, they told me how interesting they thought it was, and I had a jolly meal.

On the way up country, on the Eastern Border of Vietnam, I had with me an interpreter and a driver. We wanted to have a look at the lonely desert country and had to leave the car and walk across. I saw, ahead of us, a long line of camels with a Vietnamese man on each, and I went across the border to photograph them with my camera. This appalled the two Thais who were with me and were frightened to death of the Vietnamese camel riders. However, I continued over the border, and as the camels came, slowly, in a single line, I took pictures of them. Not one of the camel riders looked towards me, as though they thought I was some ground insect. When you think of it, I must have been like an insect when they were looking, if they had looked, from the very great height of their camels.

Full of satisfaction at my photographs, I was suddenly dreadfully afraid because my two Thai men had disappeared. All I could see was endless desert, totally unpopulated. To my utter relief, after walking and walking for half an hour, I saw a tree, and low and beyond that tree were the two Thais. They said that if the camel riders noticed them, they would have been killed.

Getting back to the car, off we went, turning north to the extreme border, beyond which was dense forest. In the forest lived primitive people whom the Thai people feared. There was a tough gamekeeper who entered the forest, and he recommended taking us in to observe the situation. Again, my two Thai helpers would not venture in. But I did, and the gamekeeper and I left the Thais in the most northerly city, and off we went. It was extremely dense, and we had to push and press our way forward and also cross streams. All at once we entered a small cleared patch and saw two little children sitting on the ground in front of a bush hut. A primitive woman emerged carrying a bowl with something in it intended for the children. Suddenly, she saw us, and instantly frightened, she dropped the bowl and ran back into the hut. The gamekeeper said we must leave, and so we struggled on in the dense forest. But we never saw another of the primitives. Back in the Thai city, I joined the interpreter and driver and we stayed on for three or four days.

The community was happy, and they busied themselves with many artistic activities. We left them, travelling down towards the centre of Thailand.

Arriving back in Bangkok, I was overcome by the charm and friendliness of the people in this garish, exuberant, bewitching capital city. The breathtaking temples, the klongs (canals) which drifted amiably along the side of streets ...

I left Bangkok for the Philippines but it was at a time when the Vietnam War was raging, so I had to change planes in Vietnam. I took a flight from Bangkok to Saigon (named Ho Chi Minh City after the end of the war). It was full of American GIs returning to the war after a respite in Thailand. They were all extremely gloomy, not wanting to have anything more to do with the conflict. Lorries had waited at Saigon for the American soldiers, who all quickly disappeared. Horrendously, I found myself completely alone in this wartime city. In the plane, I had been given coupons for meals because Vietnam had no currency during the war. But there were no restaurants, only a completely empty airport. Anxiously I waited on and on, hoping that a plane would touch down eventually. Miraculously, a French jet landed, and I urged the pilot to take me onboard – he was going to the Philippines. The Philippines were three-hundred years under the Spanish, who themselves, in 1898, were beaten by the Americans. The Americans colonised the Philippines until 1945, leaving chaos and confusion in their wake.

Chapter 8

Risk of Attack

Cosmopolitan Manila, the capital city, was enjoying the final freedom from Spain and the Second World War Japanese. A country with seven thousand isles, big and small, was an exciting place to visit, and I began travelling from the extreme north, a thousand miles down to the south. I had picked up an interpreter, Lapuz, to travel with me in the prosperous Southern State, Mindanao. We arrived at Wao, where a special luncheon had been arranged in a very large barn, with a very long table set for lunch. We began with seventeen men and myself. Each man had a gun, which he rested beside his luncheon plate. I was told that after lunch, I must travel on twelve miles through difficult country, where there may be some natives with guns coming out of the bush onto the road, and they equipped us in our jeep with four men to support us – one sitting on the running board with his gun ready, and the other three round and about the vehicle. Mercifully, we reached Banisilan without any attack on the road. The Mayor in the town of Banisilan had arranged two festivals in one day – one for the primeval people, who went back centuries in the country and possessed it as their own, and one for people who had come to live in the state from further north. It was going to take two days, and I had been given a room in a barn for the night. On being shown the room, I found it was full of marvellous antiques from the indigenous people. In the evening, they displayed before us fantastic dances in tribal dress, and when I finally went to bed, there were three primevals sitting in a circle guarding me. Amazingly, when I woke in the morning, all the beautiful objects had been removed, and the room was completely empty – the tribals who had performed the night before were completely gone.

The next evening it was the turn of the newcomers to the area. The performance was far less exciting and very modern. In the barn, I had just the bed and no pictures or decorations of any sort whatsoever. The next morning Lapuz and I returned to Manila.

One year later, I was again in South East Asia, and I paid a visit to the Philippines. I had hardly been in my room when I received a telephone call: "If you do not leave the Philippines within twenty-four hours, you will be killed."

I had arrived at Manila, the capital of the Philippines, and booked myself into a hotel for the night. Not half an hour later, the telephone rang with the threat of assassination. I was shocked and spent a very worrying night. Early next morning, I was unexpectedly visited by the driver of one of the President's cars. He said, "You are invited by the President to enjoy, with him, morning coffee." This was completely unrelated to my earlier telephone call and was a great relief. I explained to the President my reason for returning to the Philippines. During the conversation, while we were having coffee, I told him of the anxiety that I had over the telephone call. He said he had heard that very successful tribal dances were performed before me in Banisilan, in the distant state. The country was so fertile, where the tribals had been living for many centuries, that there was now tremendous fighting because the rich landlords around Manila were taking up the tribals' land, pushing them out. The tribals were strongly resisting and fighting the landlords, and my visit with the locals had angered them. "Yes," he said, "as long as you are here, you are in real danger, and they will kill you. I will give you one of the Presidential cars and a driver, which you will keep until you leave Manila."

With relief, I completed my appointments in Manila and left for the airport, anxious that I was being watched all the time. I took a flight out of the country but in fact it was a flight back to the extreme Southern State into Davao City .With amazing good fortune, I found Lapuz. Together we returned to Wao.

After a short visit, meeting again the local Mayor and senior officials, I left the country on a flight to Sarawak, Malasia. Once there, I had to be tested. Either I was to be accepted or rejected and turned out, and this was how they made their conclusion – I was to run through their longhouse, which had thirty-five individual families living in it, and I was to knock on the door of each family. If I failed before the end of the line, I would be thrown out into the river. It was an exhausting experience, but thankfully, I succeeded, and I was given a festive dinner, including snake and other local creatures, and there were a large number of the tribal people in Sarawak enjoying the great occasion.

Chapter 9

A Narrow Escape

I was back again in Africa, in troubled Sierra Leone. I had selected, at random, forty villages up and down the country to be visited, and civil war was raging in parts of the nation. It happened that one of the villages, chosen at random, to which I would visit, was right in the heart of the war zone. I had a Sierra Leone interpreter with me, and together we carried on into this particular village. It was alarming. The village contained only women, the men all being off fighting. The women were aggressive, and they attacked us. We had seen two British charity workers. The very next day after we left, the British men had been attacked and imprisoned, where they were kept for the next five months without being released. We had, mercifully, left just in time, otherwise we would also have been captured.

Travelling down on the Western side of the country, our next village had other problems. It was a small, remote place, which had no contact with the rest of the nation. We had to walk a pretty long distance to get to it, because our vehicle could not make the trip. I was approached by an elderly lady who presented me, from her two hands, five eggs. Then she enquired after the welfare of King George and Queen Mary. There appeared to have been no contact between the outside world and the village. A man walked by me holding a stick, with another man at the end of the stick who was blind. The village was overwhelmed by river blindness. A large part of Sierra Leone was either at war or suffering deadly sickness, and it had been very informative travelling over the entire country to a number of villages selected at random. Travelling on into the centre of the country, we were suddenly faced with a long line of traffic and had to enter a queue. Our driver panicked and ran away. We continued to remain in our vehicle. We could not tell what was holding us all up, until a policeman appeared at the side of the car. He, fortunately, mistook what I said, that we were employed a firm named 'Minster'. He thought I had said 'minister' and he said, "Ah, the Government. I will go back and tell the soldiers holding the cars and vehicles up." He returned and said, "You are permitted to leave the queue." We called our driver and began to drive alongside the whole line of traffic, and when we got to the end, we were suddenly faced with very bright lights. We could not see who the soldiers were as they ordered us to leave and move quickly away. As we left, we were alone on a large country road. We finally reached the city.

Chapter 10

The Unexpected

We were lounging in the garden on a fine afternoon when the postman came with a rather fantastic-looking envelope. We opened it with some eagerness, as it had 'Royal Signatories' on it. It was a letter informing me that I had been awarded an MBE.

Off we went to Buckingham Palace to receive the award, Shirley, Jane, and Paul attending. We were told that the ceremony on the day began at ten in the morning. We left home at an early hour and had a super breakfast, along with our taxi driver as a guest, in a restaurant near the Palace. So excited was the taxi driver, he missed the Palace entrance and drove us into the stable yard, which caused great anxiety, as by the time we finally reached the queue to Buckingham Palace, we almost missed the ceremony.

On entering the Palace, I was separated from Shirley, Jane and Paul and taken away into another part of the building. I entered a large room, which included many who were receiving awards. After a little time, we were taken in a long file into the Great Hall where all the visitors were seated, waiting. Then I reached my turn at the beginning of the file to stand in front of the Prince of Wales.

The Prince was acting on behalf of the Queen on this particular occasion. "Whatever are they talking about," said the listening audience. The Prince had just returned from Sierra Leone, which was engaged in civil war, where I myself had been employed, and we were deeply conversing about the serious problems facing the country. At last we reminded ourselves that we were in a public ceremony, and I stepped back a few paces.

I worried myself about curtseying, fearing that I could fall. With great effort, I managed and immediately left, but I went in the wrong direction, back towards the queue which was about to be received by the Prince. "Wrong way," said the man waiting to move forward to be the next recipient before the Prince. Half a dozen official men behind the Prince moved forward in horror as I turned and ran back past the Prince into my position.

Shirley, in her position in the audience, rose up off her chair in absolute horror also, and the Prince remained totally unmoved, quietly watching the drama. It appeared that he was well aware of Shirley's appal. Finally, as the ceremony concluded, the Prince walked up past the audience to leave the premises. He passed close by Shirley. She said, "He smiled at me."